The Complete Beginners Guide to Firearms Ownership

Glenn J Fleming Jr

Copyright © 2020 Glenn J Fleming

All rights reserved.

ISBN:

DEDICATION

This book is dedicated to all the folks who are curious about firearms. No matter if it's education on the purchase of a new gun or just a curiosity on the subject. It is my hope this book will answer questions and dispel myths.

ACKNOWLEDGMENTS

As with my other books I want to thank everyone who has inserted knowledge in the "ol' noggin". Your guidance has been invaluable, and I hope I do it justice.

1 BEFORE ALL ELSE, SAFETY

Guns, as a tool, are no more dangerous than any other inanimate object that can kill you. Indeed, they pretty much follow Newtons law, "an object at rest tends to stay at rest until acted on by an outside force". This is true with a hammer, a chainsaw, a car, or a gun.

Just like with any tool or machine there are important safety rules that should be talked about. Likening it to cars we know that you do not just go out on the road you need training before you happily drive to and fro.

Note: for the people that read this and say, "well you need a license to drive a car why don't you need one for a gun"? The answer is simple;

1. Owning a firearm is a RIGHT and that right is protected by the United States Constitution
2. Do I need a license for a chainsaw? Can it not do a significant amount of damage that?

Not a particularly good analogy but I think you get the point.
But I digress.

With gun ownership you need to realize safety is job one, and the most important and first safety rule, even if you remember no others is:

ALWAYS TREAT A GUN AS IF IT'S LOADED! EVEN IF YOU ARE SURE IT ISNT!!

I will hammer this home so many times you will be sick of it by the end of this book but if you remember that and nothing else I'll have done my job.

The second rule is:

NEVER POINT A GUN AT SOMETHING UNLESS YOU INTEND TO DESTROY IT!

This rule is important because, let's face facts, guns can do a significant amount of damage to whatever they shoot. Take this rule to heart. Incidentally, this also pretty much covers "always keep it pointed in a safe direction"

Third, and if you don't follow this one other gun owners will tease the hell out of you:

ALWAYS KEEP YOUR FINGER OFF THE TRIGGER UNTIL YOU ARE READY TO SHOOT!

These are the most basic of rules and the ones you need to commit to memory.

Now having gone over those reread them and continue.

2 WHY OWN A GUN AND WHAT SHOULD I GET?

The reasons to own a gun are as individual as the stars. Some want one for personal protection, some to protect others and still others just enjoy target shooting or just putting holes in paper. The list here is long and I'm not even going to try to cover them all. If you are reading this, and I hope you are, you have your own personal reasons and that should end the conversation.

I will say this though; There are some flat out crazy and uncaring "people" out there and while you may want a gun for other reasons, protection of yourself and your family is not a bad idea.

I personally got into guns because I thought they were cool. I was about 5 at the time, so shooting guns was a big deal! This hobby evolved into a passion and that passion turned into a profession. Something that I can now share my knowledge of and bring people into the fold and do it safely.

Let us say you have decided to buy a gun; Awesome!! Welcome to the club! Before you buy, there are a couple important things to think about.

Do you have kids? If so, you damn sure should get some sort of lock box that they cannot get to. It's not enough to just "keep a gun out of reach". Kids have the uncanny ability to get everywhere, especially where you do not want them to be. There are tons of biometric gun safes that open in a flash if it is needed. Do not get cheap on this part. Buy the absolute best lock box you can afford.

Some of you are saying "well my kid is smart, so I don't need that". That is great you have a responsible small person in the house. The trouble is some of his/her friends may be shit heads, so bear that in mind.

Another thing to think about goes back to use. Do you want a gun for home protection, for carry, for plinking, for sport, for hunting? Each purpose would require a different type of gun. I have been in this game quite a while and I cannot for the life of me think of a "one gun to rule them all" type of firearm.

So, let's break it down shall we?

"I want a gun for home protection".

This can cover a great many guns but there are a couple things to think about. Some folks will tell the aspiring gun owner that an AR15 is just the ticket for home protection. While it is a great gun, it's not suitable for firing in a home under severe stress. What if you shoot wide and miss? A 5.56 round will have no problem going through two panels of sheetrock and doing damage to what is on the other side. Of course, in all fairness so will 00 buck (shotgun ammo) or even a 9mm for that matter! This is a pretty important factor to consider with the purchase of a high-power firearm.

Hell, you may be the best shot in the world but until you are shooting for your life you have no idea what you will do, let alone how accurate you will be.

Think about it.

Someone just broke into your home and woke you from a sound sleep, you are groggy, you are scared. Are you sure it's not one of the kids? The damn dog? Does the bad guy have a weapon, a gun? Most often in times of duress your brain is going a million miles an hour and there are way too many unanswered questions. It will all come down to a split-second decision.

Are you nervous yet?

You should be. We are dealing with life and death here it's not something to take lightly. Even if you do not shoot, the bad guy may. Thinking about what CAN happen before it does is not a bad idea and is a good first step in what kind of firearm works best for you.

Now that you realize what you may deal with, what type gun do you use for home defense? I'm going to say this knowing full well that I'm agreeing with Joe Biden (and it drives me nuts) but a shotgun is my personal preference, specifically, a Remington Model 870 pump in 12ga. This is a great all-around gun with a good round. You can hunt with it, you can defend yourself with it, hell, you can even go shoot skeet with it and have some fun! The point is you get a lot of "bang for the buck" with this shotgun and the best part is they are not too expensive.

Suppose you feel or know a 12ga is a bit too much for you. That is fine, they come in other calibers as well, 20ga being a popular one. They also sell reduced recoil loads for the 12ga if you want to go that way.

While I am on the subject of shells (a shotgun round is called a "shell" by the way) there are a ton of defensive type ammo, sporting ammo, and hunting ammo. Bear in mind these will still penetrate walls but, depending on ammo, the energy is dissipated much more rapidly than using a 5.56mm for example.

Shotguns also have what's called a "choke". These can be Improved, Modified, or Cylinder. There are a few more varieties but these are the most popular. A choke is essentially a restrictive cone that squeezes the shot into a certain pattern. My recommendation is to get a shotgun with a swappable choke, that way you can have the best of all worlds. Certain chokes work better with certain types of ammo. If you don't want to mess with a choke and you just have it for home defense get a cylinder bore. Basically stated a cylinder bore doesn't have a restriction at the end of the barrel to squeeze the shot and tighten the pattern of the shot. You will get the widest spread out of your shot pattern and for close range stuff that is fine.

The downside of having a shotgun is it is longer and harder to move around in restrictive areas. Also, if you plan on locking it up it would take longer to get to than a pistol. If you want to concealed carry, trust me, a shotgun is not the way to go.

Lastly on the shotgun: They do sell shotguns with rifled barrels. Unless you want a dedicated hunting gun don't get one. The rifled barrel significantly narrows the type of ammo you can use, a lot.

Let us move to another option, the pistol. There are literally thousands of variations and types of pistols out there. I will not even try to list them all. I will, however, hit on the main types.

The most popular types of pistols fall into two categories: revolvers and pistols

Ruger LCR, this gun is a revolver but differs from other revolvers in that the hammer is not exposed. The hammer is in the hump in the top rear section. This is done to make drawing from a purse or pocket easier and snag free. This gun is a double action revolver. It fires a .38 special round

For the revolver, think the old six shooter of cowboy days, while not technically accurate you will get the idea. The difference being an old six shooter is of single action design. You must cock the hammer back after every shot in order to shoot the next round.

A revolver though is fired just by squeezing the trigger and falls into the SA/DA (Single Action/Double Action) category. The hammer is actuated and the cylinder is turned by the mechanical action of pulling the trigger. This is obviously a huge advantage over the traditional single action, that is unless you plan on meeting someone at high noon.

I should explain the SA/DA aspect a bit. Essentially a single action or SA is a gun like the old six shooters where you must cock the hammer back each time before pulling the trigger. These are usually considered more accurate as you don't have to apply so much pressure to the trigger and risk "pulling" the shot.

The double action (DA), however, means that just by pulling the trigger you can fire a round. No need to cock it in advance. These have a harder trigger pull than a SA so it is possible to pull the shot by exerting so much pressure on the trigger.

A single action/double action (SA/DA) means you have the best of both worlds. You can cock the hammer back and fire the first round then fire subsequent rounds by pulling the trigger.

One of the drawbacks to a good SA/DA revolver, as we mentioned previously, is that is has a harder trigger pull when the first round is fired versus a single action. That is because you are moving all those parts by only pulling on the trigger. That having been said the benefits far outweigh the drawbacks. Adding to it a good gunsmith can lighten the trigger pull somewhat and make it a better, smoother gun to shoot.

The other big problem with the revolvers is you are usually limited in round capacity. Often the gun only carries five or, at max eight rounds.

Now a semi auto pistol or "pistol" in the common vernacular, can be SA/DA, DA, SA, or a striker fired gun. They are semi auto guns, meaning that they fire one round with every pull of the trigger kind of like the revolvers, but they carry more ammo. The ammo is loaded into a magazine that slides into the gun. The "mag" can hold anywhere from five to thirty-two rounds depending on the gun and magazine. Of course, you won't be concealed carrying with a thirty-two round mag but they are fun if you are just "plinking". Semi-automatic pistols can also be somewhat smaller in size and deliver more "bang for the buck". Caliber selection is often better as well.

Beretta M9A3, this gun is a semi-automatic single action/double action pistol. Note the exposed hammer. It fires a 9mm bullet.

Let's look at the Beretta M9A3. An absolutely huge SA/DA pistol, not terribly suitable for concealed carry, but very good for everything else. Having a magazine capacity of 17 rounds normally, it is just a solid good gun!

This pistol has an exposed hammer that can be manually cocked to give a nice light trigger pull (SA). After the first firing the slide automatically moves to the rear and resets the hammer keeping it in SA mode.

Or it can be fired in DA by just pulling the trigger on the first round and SA on subsequent rounds.

Confused yet? In a nutshell all that stuff just means that you will be more accurate with the gun and that it can be more safely carried.

Let me explain.

We have already learned what a single action/double action (SA/DA) gun is so let's briefly talk about why that matters beyond accuracy. You would not want to carry a SA gun with the hammer back ready to fire. That is a recipe for disaster. If your parts are a little worn and the gun gets knocked it could go off. If you accidentally hit the trigger it will go off then too. A DA gun on the other hand is not always "ready to go off" the hammer is down, and it takes a bit of effort to pull the trigger to make the thing fire. It is just a safer way to carry. It can also be brought on target more quickly if needed. The SA/DA can be carried with the hammer down and be ready when needed. After you fire the first round you would then be in single action territory and it will be both easier to fire and more accurate.

Of course, there are the oddballs like the 1911. A gun that fires from single action and needs to be carried with the hammer back so it is ready to go. If you are a first-time gun owner, I strongly suggest you stay away from a 1911 purchase, no matter how many "Fudds" tell you that you need one.

By the way, a "Fudd" is a term in the gun world that has a couple meanings but basically its someone who thinks they know everything about guns but actually knows very little. They will however impart their "wrong" knowledge any time they can, to show how much they know.

Back to the 1911, and I know I'll catch hell for this but, it's an antiquated design, it's heavy, you have to have the hammer back when you carry to be ready to go, and it generally only holds seven or eight rounds. Not ideal for first time gun owner.

The last type of pistol we will talk about are the striker fired type. These would include the very popular Glocks or Smith and Wesson Shields. This type of firearm does not have an exposed hammer. Instead they have an internal mechanism that is cocked back when the trigger is pulled. This brings back a spring loaded "striker" that when it reaches its most rearward travel it is released by the sear. The striker then moves forward, under spring pressure and the firing pin portion hits the primer and fires the round.

A fifth generation Glock 17, This is a striker fired semi-automatic pistol. Note there is no hammer at all. This pistol fires a 9mm cartridge.

These have all the advantages of the SA/DA pistols, large standard mag capacity, and slim design. They also add a couple others. The trigger is generally lighter than a SA/DA gun (you can also do trigger work on them to lighten them up), there is no exposed hammer to snag on anything if drawing from concealed carry holster (think clothing snag), and they are arguably lighter than a comparable SA/DA gun.

So that is typically the three types of pistols out there. There are a ton more to be sure, but I want to keep this simple.

Lastly, we will talk about the rifle. First off repeat after me.
"An AR15 or store bought AK47, is NOT an assault rifle!"
Right off the bat I am going to say that a rifle is not a good home defense gun. They are longer than a pistol or about the same size as a shotgun. Also, the rounds are generally more powerful which is not necessarily what you want when shooting in a house with

sheetrock walls. They do however hold more rounds in the magazine than either a pistol or a shotgun. Often the standard capacity mag is 30 rounds.

You may hear that a hunting rifle is a good option as you can hunt with it as well. If you hear that from someone smile and never speak to them about guns again.

A hunting rifle is just that, for hunting. They can be bolt action, semi auto, or single shot. They use a powerful round and are long as hell. Just say no to a dedicated hunting rifle for home defense.

I'm not going to spend a lot of time here on rifles but let's just say the rifle, to my mind, is great for defense of a property or if faced with a large group of assailants but not very good for in the home.

3 SO YOU WANT A GUN, WHICH TO GET?

When I owned a gun shop, I used to see customers come in looking for their first gun with their significant other who was an "experienced" shooter. The one who did not know very much about guns would listen in awe about how they needed a colt 1911 in .45 caliber because "they don't make a .46".

The person would buy the gun, even though they were clearly nervous about the size, weight, and caliber. They would later that day go out to shoot it and try to return it the next day as it was clearly "too much gun". Even worse they would fear it and never shoot it at all!

This brings up some interesting points.

If you are trying to get someone into guns for the first time
   1. Do not force them to shoot if they do not want to. This will in no way have a positive impact on them.
   2. If they do want to shoot don't give them the largest caliber gun you own because "you think it will be funny". At this point you are just being a dickhead and you do the gun community a huge disservice. Sell your guns and start knitting.
   3. Do not force them to buy a gun because you think its what they want. Let them decide and get comfortable. If they want to later, they can check out others on your recommendation.

Now that that is out of the way, how do you pick the best gun for you?

What you want to do is go to as many gun stores as possible. Look at the different guns and get a feel for them, see which fits your hand better. If you have a range that rents guns nearby, I STRONGLY suggest that you try a couple out. If you are completely new to guns and do not feel you know what you are doing let them know. If they are any kind of good shop, they will help you out. A little later I will walk you through firing a gun for the first time. If you have a friend or significant other who has guns, ask them to take you out shooting. This can be a good way to get out of the house and get some sun and have a good time doing it!

Start off with what you are comfortable with. If recoil is a big issue for you start with a .22 caliber. These are good for getting used to firing a gun, however, not great for home defense. If you are a little more adventurous, I suggest a 9mm. It's probably the most popular caliber out there and there are a ton of different firearms you can go through to find what is right for you.
But what if you want a shotgun?

This is a little different as you will not be able to "try before you buy" at a gun range. At least I do not know of any that rent shotguns.
In a nutshell the things you will be worried about with a shotgun are length of pull, the length between the end of the buttstock to the trigger. A length of pull too long for you will make you feel "stretched" out and a length of pull (LOP) too short will leave you feeling bunched up when you hold the gun. The LOP is adjustable by either cutting the stock or adding butt pads by the way.
What gauge you are looking for? If you are recoil sensitive go with a 20ga or buy reduced recoil loads for a 12ga.
And finally, what type action you want? Semi auto shotguns are very nice and take less experience to work but they are more expensive that a pump shotgun. A pump takes a little getting used to, but they are fine guns for whatever you need them for.
Again, if you know someone who owns one ask them to take you out shooting. Maybe y'all can go to a skeet range. You probably wont hit anything your first time out but its still a lot of fun!

Looking to purchase a rifle basically is about the same as a shotgun. You probably will not find a place that rents them but its worth making some calls.
The big thing when selecting a rifle is its intended purpose. Is it

for defense, for plinking, or maybe hunting and varmint eradication are the issues?

Looking at the first reason, defense, I have said and will again that I do not really like the idea of a rifle for home defense. They just have to much penetration for a suitable home defense gun. That having been said they do serve a great many other roles. If you are just wanting to shoot cans or make holes in paper a rifle is a ton of fun. A gun that can't be beat for plinking is the Ruger 10/22. This is a handy little .22 caliber that will surely dose out the fun. When you are ready for it, buy an AR15 and have more fun at longer ranges.

Obviously for hunting you will want a bigger caliber rifle. At that point recoil comes into play as the bigger in caliber you go the harsher the recoil will be. There are only about 20 million different hunting guns out there, it would be a fool's errand to list them. I will go back to the AR15 though. For smaller animals or varmints this is a great gun!

Long story short on this topic you will have to decide what type gun you want and what fits your needs. Just remember if you are brand new to the sport try out as many as you can. Do not settle for something that is "good enough". There are a lot of different choices and you will find one that fits you

Next, I'll cover what to do when you want to buy one.

4 WELCOME TO THE FOLD NEW GUN OWNER

So, you have made your choice and you want a gun.

What can you expect when buying?

First off bring your ID to the gun shop. Even if you bought it online you will have to do a background check and produce ID. Yep you WILL have to do a background check! Contrary to what the media tells you if you buy a gun you will have to do a background check. All the talking heads spouting off about the "gun show loophole" are pretty much just full of BS.

Sorry I'm not trying to have any kind of political slant to this book but sometimes its hard.

Anyway, when you go to the gun show or gun shop you will need to fill out what is called an ATF form 4473. This is basically the form that asks if you are a felon, fugitive from justice, or a domestic abuser. Marking in the affirmative on either of these questions, as well as some others, will put you in the DENIED category and you will not be able to buy a gun. Make sure you read ALL the questions and answer truthfully. Not doing so is a felony!

Now that you have filled out the 4473 what happens next. An employee of the gun shop will call the FBI NICS line to tell them the info on your 4473. They run a quick background check and if you pass you can then legally buy the gun.

There are a couple caveats to this though. Sometimes you will get delayed. This actually happens a lot and doesn't mean you can't buy a gun it just means the FBI has to look a little farther into it. This may be because you may have the same name as Joe Bob the felon or a host of other reasons. Sometimes the more extensive check takes a couple minutes, sometimes a couple days. In most cases, if the shop does not hear back with a denial you can pick your gun up in few days. This may vary from shop to shop though.

If you bought a gun online you will still need to go through a local FFL to have the background check done once the gun arrives, by mail, to the gun shop. In most cases there will be a $25-$50 charge for running the background check if you bought online.

If you have any questions on the firearm you are buying, make sure to hit up the employee to help you out. They are sure to be of service to you.

So now you have a gun, where do you go from here?

I know you are itching to go shoot but I suggest you bring the firearm home and do a little familiarization with it. Once home take it out of the case and make sure it's not loaded (remember our first rule) then read the owner's manual that came with the gun. They are more specific on your new firearm than I will ever be. Next you will find a gun lock in the box. It's required by law that one comes with each new gun. It's a key lock with a loop on it. Unless you need a key lock with a loop on it for your bicycle or such, gently take it to the kitchen and throw it in the trash. It is the single most useless thing ever found to be "necessary" in the history of the world.

Hey if you have kids, you did get a biometric safe right?

After that, when pointed in a safe direction, go ahead and hold the gun like you are going to shoot it. You can even go "pew pew" if you want to.

Rack the slide back, if so equipped, or if it's a revolver release the cylinder (the part where the bullets go) and check it out. For rifles or shotguns again read the manual and familiarize yourself with your new firearm. The important thing to remember when getting used to your new firearm is to always treat it as if its loaded and always point it in a safe direction. Dry firing is acceptable unless its an older gun or a .22 caliber. Dry firing some of those can be detrimental to the gun.

Once you are familiar with the manual and the feel of the gun its ready to go to the range.

I can't stress this point enough, if you are still unsure or apprehensive about the gun, bring a friend who is "gun savvy" with you to help you out. If you don't have someone like that schedule yourself a class to become familiar with both your gun and range etiquette. In fact, I recommend taking a class whether you have friends who are gun people or not. You can usually talk to your local shop and if they don't have classes, they can hook you up with one.

These classes will help you become more comfortable with your new purchase. They will go over how to use it, proper hold, loading, etc. and may even go over cleaning. They should also go over range rules. They do vary from range to range, but the basic ones are all the same. If you can't find either a friend or a class have no fear, I'll go over that in subsequent chapters.

In fact, let's do that now.

5 GUN RANGE RULES

As I alluded to earlier, range rules will vary from range to range, especially if you are in an indoor versus outdoor range. Let's cover the most basic one. Never go to the range with an already loaded gun. At best this is an unsafe practice. At worse it can be a dangerous practice. Take your gun, unloaded, in the case to the range. If it's a range with employees, you may be asked to show the gun to make sure its unloaded. This is a pretty common practice and not one to be troubled over.

While I'm on the subject of ranges I should say that most indoor ranges will not allow rifles or shotguns to be fired in their ranges.

Put on your ear and eye protection (you did remember those right?) and proceed to the range itself.

Go to your firing lane and set up. They will usually have a tabletop or shelf that you can set your stuff on.

At this point you will want to set up your targets. If its an indoor range they will often have an electrical system where you do not have to go down range to set up your targets. If it's an outdoor range or if they don't have the new-fangled electric set up calmly wait till the range line is called "cold", this means no one will be shooting. It also means don't mess with your gun! There is a nothing more annoying than being downrange and having someone play with a gun behind your back. Did I mention it's a huge safety violation as well?

Once your target is set up and both everyone is back from down range and the range is called hot, it's time to load up.
Take your gun and load it. You can load with one round or the max number it will hold. It's up to you.

At this point you have a loaded firearm and must act accordingly. There should be no horse play, no waving it around or pointing in an unsafe direction. You should shoot at the target and only the target.

Take your firing stance, aim and slowly squeeze the trigger. Make holes in the paper and have fun. Reload and have more fun.

But wait! We forgot to go over stance and aiming. That would help huh.

6 THE BASICS, PROPER SHOOTING GRIP AND STANCE

In this chapter we are going to cover the basics of shooting. How to hold the gun and how to stand when firing. These are pretty important details as if you aren't holding the gun correctly there are a few things that can happen. One of those things is the gun can fly out of your hand! This of course, is dangerous as when it flies out of your hand then hits the ground there is the possibility of the gun going off again. At this point no one knows what direction the bullet will take, not the best of things to happen to be sure. The second thing that will happen is that everyone around you will start laughing at you. You may even end up on a video going viral!

Another thing that can happen with a poor grip involves semi autos. You can run the risk of getting a nasty cut on your hand if your grip is too high. This is because when the slide moves to the rear it will not know, or care, that part of your hand is in the way. This, in turn, leads to a new scar. I know, chicks dig scars, right? But that doesn't mean you necessarily want a new one.

The method of holding a firearm varies from gun to gun, but not much. Mostly the variations are in the grip angle or type of pistol grip. These have to do with the design of the gun, and you don't have much control over that, save buying a gun you find comfortable.

All the examples here are going to be with right hand grip for a right-hand shooter. If you are a "lefty" simply reverse the actions I am showing you and press on.

You will want to take the gun, by the grip in your right hand, ensure it is unloaded when you are practicing this. Now extend your right hand in front of you, bringing the gun up to your eye level. You can shoot like this but a way to shoot more accurately is to take your left hand and cup it around your right.

Make sure you aren't locking your elbows.
Both thumbs should be on the same side and should be pointing forward. It should feel comfortable and provide a solid base for shooting. If it feels a little weird you can adjust as necessary to get a better grip. When holding the gun don't just lightly grasp it, by the same token don't try to strangle it either. Your grip should be firm yet have a little "flex" to it. It takes a bit of practice to get the grip down but once you have it, you will know. It will just feel sort of natural and comfortable.

Proper hold technique, notice the left hand is cupping the right hand. Essentially you "push out" with the right hand and "pull back" with the left hand. Photo credit, Hikari Fleming

Of course, there are many different methods to holding a pistol, but this is the most basic and will get you by till you want to experiment on others.

Stance is a little bit more flexible. I'll cover two that I use and find comfortable.

The first is standing with feet, about shoulder width apart, facing the target. This is called the Isosceles shooting stance. You want to have a slight flex in your knees and hips. The reason you don't want to stand ram rod straight is because your balance won't be as good when faced with the recoil of the gun. This should feel pretty natural to you and will provide a nice stable platform.

Isosceles shooting stance as viewed head on.

Isosceles shooting stance as viewed the side.

The things to remember are, don't lean forward to much and don't lean back at all.

The second stance is standing with your feet, again shoulder width apart, but this time you face your left shoulder towards the target (right shoulder for left-handed shooters). This is called the weaver stance. Your left foot should basically be pointing at the target. Your right or rearward foot should be kicked back and your foot angled almost, 45 degrees in relation to your left foot. Again, maintain a slight bend in your knees and waist. Lean slightly forward but not too far forward, just as in the Isosceles shooting stance.

Weaver stance as viewed from the front

Weaver stance as viewed from the side.

For Rifle or shotgun hold the stances would be the same. The caveat here is you would want to lean into it slightly more. This will help you maintain balance when faced with the recoil when shooting this type of firearm. Of course the particular hold on the gun would vary due to the design of the long gun but in general you want your right hand (for right handed shooters) on the pistol grip or grip on the buttstock and your left hand farther up on the forearm.

Profile view of the Weaver stance with a Remington 870. Notice Im leaning slightly forward. Photo credit Brandon Riley

Weaver shotgun stance as viewed from the 11 o'clock of the shooter. Photo Credit Brandon Riley

7 AIMING AND FIRING

Aiming a gun is basically lining up the front and rear sight and pointing them, accurately, at the target. The sights consist of a front "blade" and a rear "notch". There are many variations of sights out there red dot scopes, reflex, peep. The list is long, but we will focus on the standard open iron sights.

Your front sight will be a raised "blade" your rear sight will consist of another blade turned 90 degrees to the front sight that has a notch cut into it. Sometimes there is just a notch. Either way it serves the same purpose. Your task at hand is to line up the sights so that the front sight is aligned with the rear sight so that they form a complete flat line.

In other words, put the front sight in the notch on the rear sight and make them flat on top.

When you are using your sights make sure your front sight is clear, meaning not fuzzy. Your rear sight should be a little fuzzy as you focus on the front.

This can be achieved with either one eye or both eyes open. I happen to shoot with both eyes open.

Here you can see proper sight alignment. Notice the front sight is clear and the rear sight is a bit fuzzy. By the way, this picture was a real pain to take.

Of course, there may be an issue here as well because things are never simple. You may find that you are cross eye dominant.

In other words, you do everything right-handed but are left eye dominant. An easy way to tell if you are is this simple test.

1. Extend your arms out in front of you and create a triangular opening between your thumbs and forefingers by placing your hands together at a 45-degree angle.
2. With both eyes open, center this triangular opening on a distant object.
3. Close your left eye.
4. If the object stays centered, your right eye (the one that is open) is your dominant eye. If the object is no longer framed by your hands, your left eye is your dominant eye.

So, let's say that you now know you are left eye dominant, what do you do? Unfortunately, I haven't found a good method to overcome this other than to shoot left-handed or to just accept it. There may be other methods but like I said, I haven't found it yet.

Getting back to shooting. Once you have achieved your proper sight picture and you are aiming at the target its time to fire the gun.

In this I am assuming the gun is in a condition to fire. By this I mean you have previously loaded the gun, the hammer (if equipped) is back on a loaded chamber and the safety is off.

Place your finger on the trigger, proper placement being on the pad between the front of your finger and the first joint. Inhale and slowly partially exhale. Hold your breath at the midpoint of your exhalation, and slowly squeeze the trigger. Don't jerk on it, squeeze to rapidly, or take to long. The former will cause you to "pull" your shot. The latter will cause you to pass out from lack of oxygen. Keep squeezing until you hear a loud bang, it should surprise you if you are doing it right.

You have just fired a gun.

Keep your trigger finger in the rearward position after you shoot. Take a second and let the trigger move forward.

Now place the gun on safe and safely unload the gun. Place it on the shelf in front of you and pat yourself on the back.

That wasn't so hard was it?

Did you like it? Was it fun? I'll bet it was. Don't worry if you are still a bit nervous, that happens. After all the first time you rode a bike without training wheels I'll bet you were still nervous the second time around.

Training tip: The reason I had you apply the safety and unload after the first shot is to get you used to doing it. Practice this as often as you like, in a safe setting. Eventually you will work up a muscle memory on this and it will get much smoother and faster. Don't be in a hurry for that though. Make sure you are doing it correctly and speed will come. You can practice all this without having the gun loaded by the way. That way you can practice safing the gun at home while you watch Rick and Morty!

Focusing on the range again (after all you are here and you have ammo), lets reload the gun and shoot some more. This time instead of safing the gun up after your shot when you release the trigger, do your breathing and let fly with another shot. Repeat this till you have expended all ammo in the gun.

If, when you are done shooting, you hit the target more than you missed good work! If you missed, a lot, don't worry. Proper aiming takes a time and add to it you are (probably) a new shooter and are a bit nervous. I'll let you in on a gun secret. Most people, no matter how much of a gun expert they are miss once in a while, and when they were starting out, they missed a lot. Hell, I miss most of the time! I pretty much just shoot machine guns so my gun skills with single shots are pretty woeful. That having been said I am a firm believer in accuracy by volume!

.

8 SO NOW YOU'RE A SHOOTER

Congratulations on your first "range day"! All that preparation paid off didn't it? So now that you are an accomplished shooter you will need to take care of some stuff. One of the things you will be responsible for is cleaning of your new firearm. Here is another secret.

I don't clean my guns every time I shoot. There is simply no need to. I simply clean when its necessary. How often is that? Well it depends on the gun, ammo used, and the way its stored. I'll explain it a little better for you.

Some guns have a natural tendency to get dirty. There is always a small amount of carbon that builds up from firing a gun and some guns just like to hold on to that carbon more than others. If the slide or cylinder feels gummy, it's time to clean. Another way you can check, before it gets to the gummy point, is just to look at the parts when you open the action. Are they caked with grime? Are the parts that should be silver now black? Yep time to clean.

As to the ammo aspect, some ammo is just naturally dirtier than others. They leave a bigger carbon residue than others. Again, open the action and look.

Lastly the way its stored. What the hell do I mean there? Well if you store it in your fancy new lock box or the box it came in there shouldn't be a real reason for it to get dirty there, so it won't affect it much. If you store it under your bed and the dust bunnies do their job you will need to clean more often. Especially if you are one of those folks that oil the hell out of it. Oil is a natural attractant to dust bunnies, it's science!

Now the whole reason I wrote this chapter.
If you carry your gun, especially in your pocket, it will get dirty! I've seen many carry guns come in that are absolutely filthy. The owner never took the time to clean them believing that since it was not used its not dirty. Your carry gun is there to save your life if needed. Take care of it and when the time comes it will take

care of you!

9 AMMUNITION TYPES

The only thing more confusing than selecting a gun is selecting an ammo type. There are hundreds of ammo types and that's just taking into account one caliber!

Ammo selection will, of course, depend on what you are using it for. For plinking or target shooting, ball ammo will do fine.

Ball ammunition is just a lead slug encased in a copper jacket. Its good for making holes in stuff but not much else. You don't want to use it for self-defense or hunting.

The issue with ball ammo in these scenarios is that they have limited expansion. In other words, small hole in, small hole out. That's a pretty basic way of stating things but it's not too far from the truth. In a defensive situation you want a bullet that will have good penetration and good expansion. The bullet should maintain close to its original weight when hitting a target. This helps with penetration. The weight helps the bullet go deeper. In the case of expansion, that will give the maximum damage as it travels through the target. I won't go into detail on which ammo is the better as there are just too many, but a quick internet search will give you what you need. On a related note there are some semi-automatic guns that will not reliably feed some hollow point rounds. With new guns this is less of an issue, but it can happen. Unfortunately, there is no guide to select what bullet will work with what gun so it's a trial and error sort of thing.

For hunting guns bullet selection is essentially the same. You want a bullet that will hold its weight and have good expansion. The reason for this is that it is more humane in dispatching the animal.

Now shotgun ammo is a different thing. Again, there are tons of types of ammo, but for defensive use, 00 buck shot would be the ticket. Bird shot would be too light and not give good penetration and a slug would be overkill. No pun intended.

10 ACCESSORIES

I'm not going to hit these hard as there are a wonderful selection of all types of stuff out on the market, but I will hit a couple things that I think will help new shooters.

The first is lights and lasers. These are great devices to have, especially in a dark room defensive scenario. Most new guns will have what's called an accessory rail on them. These will assist in attaching said lights and lasers. Simply attach them to the rail and boom, you are in business. In a darkened room, a good light is indispensable. Most of them activate by a simple touch of the finger. Of course, lights work both ways so keep that in mind. Lasers are a very good idea for quick target acquisition. Again, simply touch it with your finger or in some cases they activated by merely gripping the gun and if it's been properly sighted in, where the laser goes the bullet goes. They even make some models that have a light and a laser in them!

Now holsters are a different story. There are so many on the market it would take a book just to cover them but to name a few types there are in the waistband (IWB), outside the waist band (OWB), shoulder, ankle; I think you are starting to get the idea. A holster is a very personal choice and generally the only way you will find your "perfect" holster is to start trying them out. I've been through many, many holsters trying to find the right one. I'll buy one, check it out for a bit by wearing it and if it doesn't fit my needs, sell it and buy a different one. It can be exhausting, especially when you consider that you have to do this for each type gun you have! I will say this though. When you select a holster make sure it is a good solid one with good retention. You don't want a flimsy holster that the top flops around. This can get lodged in the trigger guard and actually fire the gun when inserting it into the holster. On the retention side, you don't want a holster that will let the gun fall out of it. This of course, as they say in the gun world, is bad.

Lastly there are some accessories out there that amount to money thrown away. Take for example the pistol bayonet. This absolutely has to be a joke, but they don't market it that way. In short, if it looks stupid, it probably is.

Now onward to long guns again. When looking at accessories for your rifle or shotgun, to name a few, there are slings; three-point, single-point, and dual-point. There are lights/lasers. There are different buttstock, and different grips. There are things to help with closing the bolt or opening the bolt. Different muzzle devices, and about a million types of rails. Basically, go to the beach and start counting sand, that will give you some idea of how many long gun accessories there are

One good thing though. You can legitimately mount your bayonet on them and not get laughed at.... much.

11 CLOSING THOUGHTS

You may have noticed this isn't a very long book. There is a reason for that. I in no way wanted this to overwhelm new shooters. To me it just didn't make sense to write a four-hundred-page book that by the end of it the reader would forget what was in the first chapter, which was the most important part! Think of this as a reference manual. Something you can easily find the info in if you are seeking it.

I encourage you to seek knowledge on the internet as well. There are many sites dedicated to this hobby and more info than you will ever need. Once you have found your "perfect gun" go hit up YouTube. I guarantee there will be a video on maintenance and upkeep of your firearm, something that I just cannot do here as there are too many possibilities.

When you are ready join a club, do so and get to know other shooters. They will be more than glad to help you out and further your knowledge. Joining the NRA (National Rifle Association), or GOA (Gun Owners of America) isn't a bad idea as well. There are people out there that think the average person shouldn't be trusted with a firearm. They also think the founding fathers were wrong to make it a right in constitutional form. Joining these groups will let your voice be heard in the matter.

I've been shooting for a long time. I find it both enjoyable and relaxing. True if you are new, "relaxing" may be a stretch until you get some range time under your belt, but I'll bet you are having fun.

If you are, then I have done my job.

ABOUT THE AUTHOR

Born in Valdosta Ga. The author has been active in the gun community since he was five years old. He has been servicing all manner of weaponry and instructing new shooters for over a decade.

www.ingramcontent.com/pod-product-compliance
Lightning Source LLC
Chambersburg PA
CBHW041757040426
42446CB00005B/240